I0759909

This book belongs to

For you
—T. N. T.

For Mom, who gifted me her love of poetry
—J. O.

Published in the United States 2025 by Nosy Crow Inc.
145 Lincoln Road, Lincoln, MA, 01773, USA

Published in the United Kingdom by Nosy Crow Ltd.
Wheat Wharf, 27a Shad Thames, London, SE1 2XZ, UK

www.nosycrow.us

ISBN 979-8-88777-204-2

Library of Congress Catalog Card Number pending.

Printed in Shenzhen, China, following rigorous ethical sourcing standards.

1 3 5 7 9 10 8 6 4 2

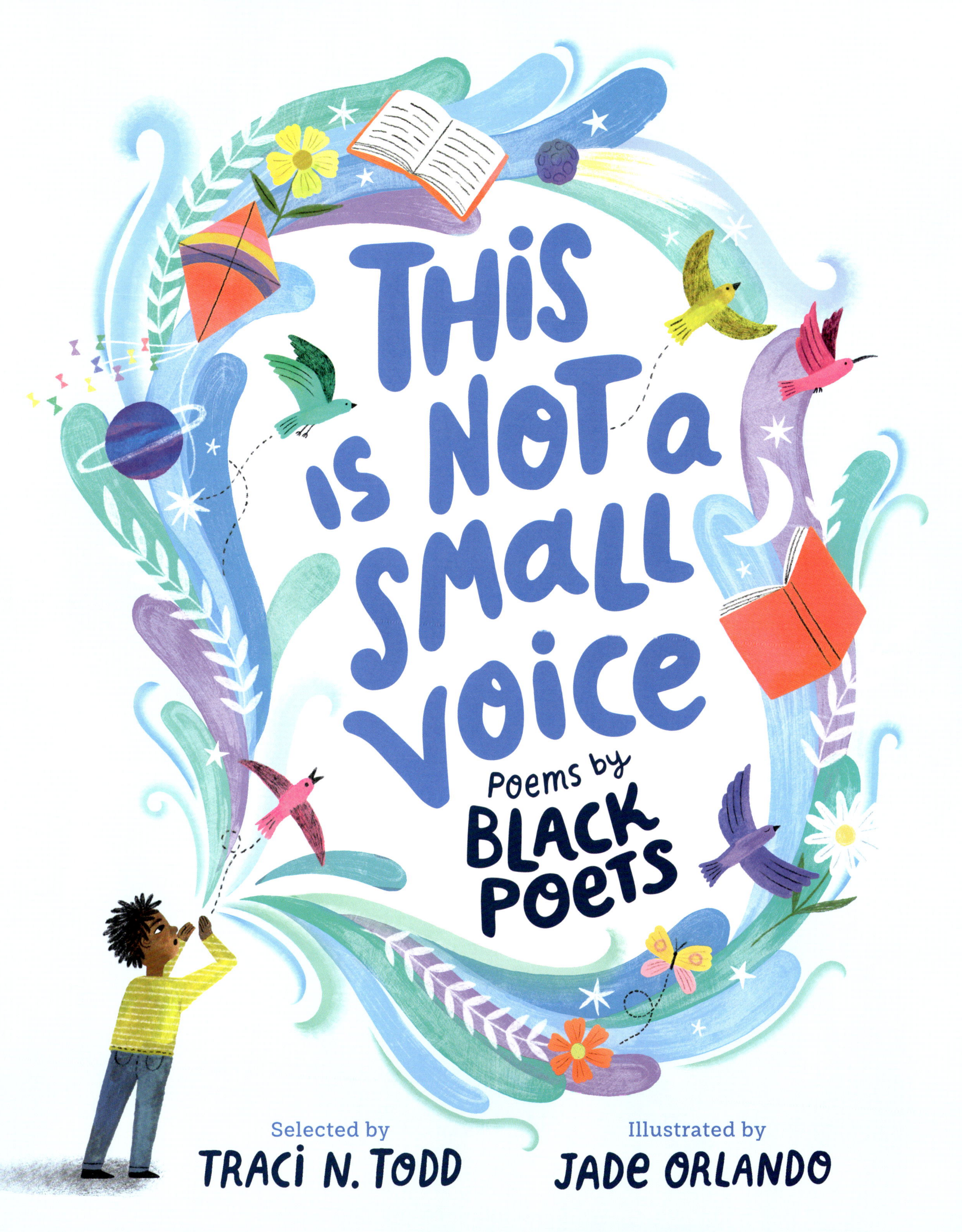
THIS IS NOT A SMALL VOICE
Poems by
BLACK POETS
Selected by
TRACI N. TODD
Illustrated by
JADE ORLANDO

INTRODUCTION

Here are two things to know about me.

First, I came into this world on the lines of a poem. I was born in Chicago in the middle a sticky, sweaty summer. I was a big baby, my mother was a small woman, and she was uncomfortably hot waiting for me to arrive. To cool herself, she recited "Stopping by Woods on a Snowy Evening" by Robert Frost over and over again. Do you know it? It starts like this:

Whose woods these are I think I know.
His house is in the village though;
He will not see me stopping here
To watch his woods fill up with snow.

Can you imagine how that poem might make you feel on a sticky, sweaty day?

Second, when I was small, my father made me memorize poems and recite them out loud. Most of the poems came from a book called *Black Voices*. I still remember the black-and-white cover and the first lines of "Mother to Son" by Langston Hughes:

Well, son, I'll tell you:
Life for me ain't been no crystal stair.

In the poem, the mother tells her son never to give up; if she's strong enough to make it, he is too. I didn't understand that when I learned the words, but I understand it now. Poems can be like that—secrets that reveal themselves over time.

My father wanted me to know Black poets, and through them, to know myself. He planted seeds early and watched them bloom. Now it's my turn in the garden.

I wanted the poems in this book to be a celebration of Blackness. And while it is impossible to capture all the things Blackness can be, I had a few ideas about where to start:

Blackness is fire
We are children of the sun
We are indigo children
And red clay children
And silt and sand and loam
Foundational

We are ocean born
And ocean claimed
Sky folk
Hope

Our hair our hands our minds
Have more beauty than words can carry
even the words we invent ourselves
and we are *always* inventing

We laugh at boxes on government forms
At language with one set of rules
We are the rules
We are no rules
We are improvisation, poetry, jazz, rhythm and rhyme
Rock and roll
Call, response
and blues
We are song and dance and drum
We are beyond imagining
Dream children
Beloved and
Our lives matter

The poets in this collection are from many different countries and cultures. Their work spans decades—and not nearly enough languages. You'll find words like *Negro* and *colored* and *black* with a lowercase *b*. What we call ourselves depends on the time, the place, and our mood.

There are all kinds of poems here—haiku and hip hop and anthems and prayers and jump rope rhymes and personal memories and universal truths. There is *a lot* of truth in these pages—I think poets are better at telling the truth than just about anyone. But this book can't contain everything or everybody. What's missing? *Who's* missing? Can you fill in the gaps?

Not all of these poems were written for children, but I think you'll still find magic in them. I encourage you to visit them again and again. Some of these poems are brand new, written specifically for this collection by Derrick Barnes, Winsome Bingham, Rio Cortez, Nikki Grimes, Ella McLeod, and Alicia D. Williams. All of these poets have much more to say. And they have friends. I hope you'll seek them out.

Now, are you ready? Are your eyes open? Your ears? Your heart?

Ours is not a small voice. I invite you to listen.

Traci N. Todd
September 2025

THE DREAM KEEPER

Bring me all of your dreams,
You dreamers.
Bring me all of your
Heart melodies
That I may wrap them
In a blue cloud-cloth
Away from the too rough fingers
Of the world.

Langston Hughes

COME ALL YOU LITTLE PERSONS

From above earth, from above sky,
from below earth, from under water,
come all you little persons
come exactly as you are.

Come little bird-person
in feathered cape.
Come little fish-person
in blouse of scales.
Come little tree-person
in robe of leaves.
Come little snake-person
in sheddable sleeves.
Come little wave-person
in shirt made of spray.
Come little mouse-person
in Sunday-best grey.
Come little moon-person
in apron that shines.
Come little bat-person
in cape of night-time.

Come little star-person
in five-pointed crown.
Come little wind-person
in invisible gown.
Come little sun-person
in dazzling tiara.
Come little bee-person
in fairy-light attire.
You too little stone-person
in rags of molten fire.

Come all you little persons
come join the dance of
Earth's guests.
Just follow your heart-song
when next it calls.
Planet Earth has room for the
footsteps of all.

John Agard

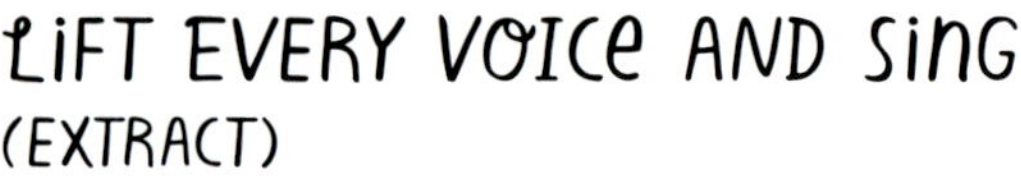

LIFT EVERY VOICE AND SING
(EXTRACT)

Lift every voice and sing
Till earth and heaven ring,
Ring with the harmonies of Liberty;
Let our rejoicing rise
High as the listening skies,
Let it resound loud as the rolling sea.
Sing a song full of the faith that the dark past has taught us,
Sing a song full of the hope that the present has brought us.
Facing the rising sun of our new day begun,
Let us march on till victory is won.

James Weldon Johnson

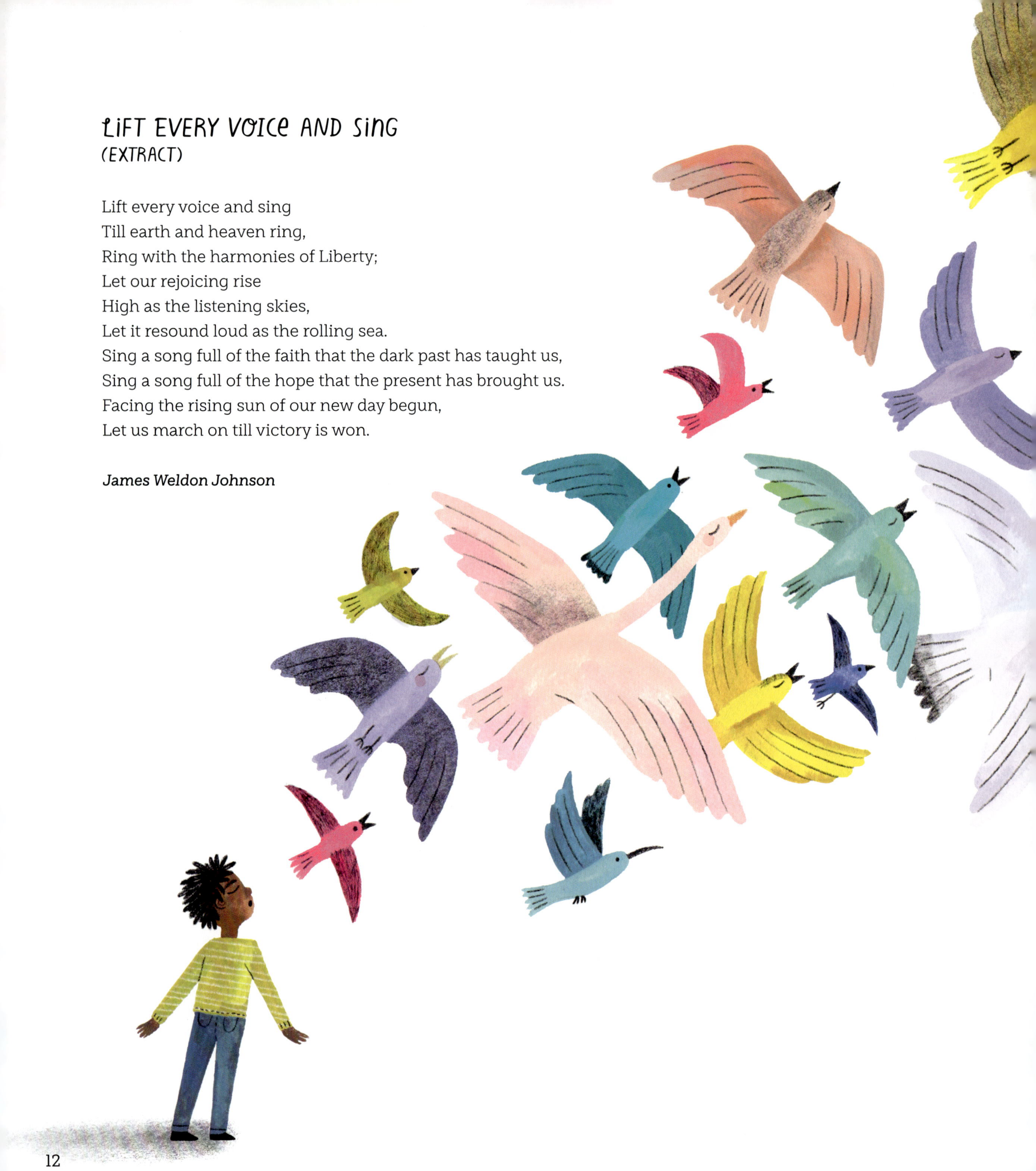

DARK TESTAMENT
(EXTRACT)

Give me a song of hope
And a world where I can sing it.
Give me a song of faith
And a people to believe in it.
Give me a song of kindliness
And a country where I can live it.
Give me a song of hope and love
And a brown girl's heart to hear it.

Pauli Murray

THIS BODY II

My body is
perfect and
imperfect and
Black and
girl and
big and
thick hair and
short legs and
scraped knee and
healed scar and
heart beating and
hands that hold and
voice that bellows and
feet that dance and
arms that embrace and
my momma's eyes and
my daddy's smile and
my grandma's hope and

my body is masterpiece and
my body is mine.

Renée Watson and Ellen Hagan

MORNING LITURGY
(EXTRACT)

There is so much beauty within
beauty attached to my names
beauty attached to my skin
beauty attached to the grace in my walk
beauty attached to my tongue
beauty attached to my flaws
look at me, brewing stars in my skin.

Ijeoma Umebinyuo

NARCISSA

Some of the girls are playing jacks.
Some are playing ball.
But small Narcissa is not playing
Anything at all.

Small Narcissa sits upon
A brick in her back yard
And looks at tiger-lilies,
And shakes her pigtails hard.

First she is an ancient queen
In pomp and purple veil.
Soon she is a singing wind.
And, next, a nightingale.

How fine to be Narcissa,
A-changing like all that!
While sitting still, as still, as still,
As anyone ever sat!

Gwendolyn Brooks

ROBERT, WHO IS OFTEN A STRANGER TO HIMSELF

Do you ever look in the looking-glass
And see a stranger there?
A child you know and do not know,
Wearing what you wear?

Gwendolyn Brooks

DON'T CRY CATERPILLAR

Don't cry, Caterpillar,
Caterpillar, don't cry.
You'll be a butterfly—by and by.

Caterpillar, please
Don't worry 'bout a thing.

"But," said Caterpillar,
"Will I still know myself—in wings?"

Grace Nichols

MUMBLE THE MAGIC WORDS

Come, claim your wings.
Lift your life above the earth,
return to the land of your father's birth.

Come, unbend your back.
Let us fade together in a trick of light.
Let us gather stars and ride the night,
never forgetting those who've forgotten
beneath the lash and sting of cotton.

kum kunka yali,
kum . . . tambe!
buba yali
buba tambe

Mumble the magic words.
Seize the sky as soaring birds.

Jabari Asim

MISS MARY MACK INTRODUCES HER WINGS

My name is Miss Mary Mack Mack Mack
you sing it my name
I turned into a bluebird last summer, I flew
through all the South. My wings are blue
and I touch the sky.
At first, I decided I was never coming back.
I took off my black
housedress. I knew freedom
was not the act of flying,
but the steady beat of wings.
It was my steady black,
blue and my blues were gone,
I wanted to be
a bird and became.

Tyree Daye

BIRD'S NEST

After Max Sansing

when daddy says my head is a bird's
nest, he means a momma bird might find it
inviting. my hair: a place to raise her first eggs,
a place her first babes might call out to her, a place
she might fly back to from the wet morning dirt, chewing
a worm in the side of her cheek, so her baby might swallow
it down easy, so her baby might fall asleep with a full stomach
and never dream of falling, so i might rise from sleep
on a Sunday morning, come downstairs dressed
for church with a head full of morning songs,
uncombed hair, hear my daddy chuckle,
search for words, and call it wild

Jamila Woods

GRANNY GRANNY PLEASE COMB MY HAIR

Granny, Granny, please comb my hair.
You always take your time,
You always take such care.

You put me on a cushion between your knees
You rub a little coconut oil,
Parting gentle as a breeze.

Mummy, Mummy,
She's always in a hurry-hurry.
Rush,
She pulls my hair.
Sometimes she tugs.

But Granny,
You have all the time
In the world
And when you're finished,
You always turn my head and say
"Now who's a nice girl?"

Grace Nichols

BEFORE GOING TO THE BARBERSHOP

I gotta call my barber Eric to
let him know I'm pullin' up. *Yo hello?*
Yea yea who this? Ahhhh yo what up homie?
How you been kid? Would say he asks a lot
of questions for a barber but he been
linin' me up 'fore I knew who I was.
I asked for stars and two lines on both sides
of my head in middle school. I asked to
keep the stars unfinished. I asked to see
the mirror and as botched as I had been—
'cause I ain't let him finish—he and I
knew this was the first time I got to choose
how I looked and since I was told not to
call a boy beautiful, I was my first.

Gabriel Ramirez

THE BLACK FLAMINGO
(EXTRACT)

I am the black flamingo.
The black flamingo is me
trying to find myself.
This book is a fairy tale
in which I am the prince
and the princess. I am
the king and the queen.
I am my own wicked
witch and fairy godmother.

This book is a fairy tale
in which I'm cursed
and blessed by others.

But, finally, I am the fairy
finding my own magic.

Dean Atta

GEL

I LIKE TO STAY UP

I like to stay up
and listen
when big people talking
jumbie stories

I does feel
so tingly and excited
inside me

But when my mother say
“Girl, time for bed”

Then is when
I does feel a dread

Then is when
I does jump into me bed

Then is when
I does cover up
from me feet to me head

Then is when
I does wish I didn’t listen
to no stupid jumbie story

Then is when I does wish I did read
me book instead

“Jumbie” is a Guyanese word for “ghost”.

Grace Nichols

ANANCY

Anancy is a spider;
Anancy is a man;
Anancy's West Indian
And West African.

Sometimes, he wears a waistcoat;
Sometimes, he carries a cane;
Sometimes, he sports a top hat;
Sometimes, he's just a plain,
Ordinary, black, hairy spider.

Anancy is vastly cunning,
Tremendously greedy,
Excessively charming,
Hopelessly dishonest,
Warmly loving,
Firmly confident,
Fiercely wild,
A fabulous character,
Completely out of our mind
And out of his, too.

Anancy is a master planner,
A great user
Of other people's plans;
He pockets everybody's food,
Shelter, land, money, and more;
He achieves mountains of things,
Like stolen flour dumplings;
He deceives millions of people,
Even the man in the moon;
And he solves all the mysteries
On earth, in air, under sea.

And always,
Anancy changes
From a spider into a man
And from a man into a spider
And back again
At the drop of a sleepy eyelid.

Andrew Salkey

AH WAS READIN' A BOOK

Ah was readin' a book about chestnut,
An' me start wonder as me a-read,
If dem roast the chestnut the same way
That we roast we jackfruit seed.

Ah was readin' a book about daffodil,
An' a thought jus' come into me head,
Yuh think the daffodil look like we mimosa,
Only yellow, instead of red?

Ah was readin' a book about motorway,
Long, wide road that don't have much ben',
An' ah wonder if them was anyt'ing like
The road between Kingston an' May Pen.

Ah was readin' a book about the Queen,
An' ah think, it would be funny,
If the English queen was a warrior,
Like we own maroon queen, Nanny.

Ah was readin' a book about England,
An' a stop an' wonder for a minute,
If a English girl have a book 'bout Jamaica,
An' if a little girl like me was in it.

Valerie Bloom

WHY SOME PEOPLE BE MAD AT ME SOMETIMES

they ask me to remember
but they want me to remember
their memories
and i keep on remembering
mine.

Lucille Clifton

Checking Out Me History

Dem tell me
Dem tell me
Wha dem want to tell me

Bandage up me eye with me own history
Blind me to me own identity

Dem tell me bout 1066 and all dat
dem tell me bout Dick Whittington and he cat
But Touissant L'Ouverture
no dem never tell me bout dat

Toussaint
a slave
with vision
lick back
Napoleon
battalion
and first Black
Republic born
Toussaint de thorn
to de French
Toussaint de beacon
of de Haitian Revolution

Dem tell me bout de man who discover de balloon
and de cow who jump over de moon
Dem tell me bout de dish run away with de spoon
but dem never tell me bout Nanny de maroon

Nanny
See-far woman
of mountain dream
fire-woman struggle
hopeful stream
to freedom river

Dem tell me bout Lord Nelson and Waterloo
but dem never tell me bout Shaka de great Zulu
Dem tell me bout Columbus and 1492
but what happen to de Caribs and de Arawaks too

Dem tell me bout Florence Nightingale and she lamp
and how Robin Hood used to camp
Dem tell me bout ole King Cole was a merry ole soul
but dem never tell me bout Mary Seacole

From Jamaica
she travel far
to the Crimean War
she volunteer to go
and even when de British said no
she still brave the Russian snow
a healing star
among the wounded
a yellow sunrise
to the dying

Dem tell me
Dem tell me wha dem want to tell me
But now I checking out me own history
I carving out me identity

John Agard

WAVES

There are waves to chase and waves that crash,
There are waves to jump like skipping ropes,
Waves to run away to sand, waves to leap and bound.
Waves that are turquoise, waves that are brown,
Waves full of seaweed, waves that drown.
Waves clear and calm, waves angry and wronged,
Waves that whisper, waves that roar like thunder,
Waves you'd never swim under, pounding rocks and shore.

Waves that put you to sleep, sssh sssh sssh cradle-rock.
Waves that look like sea horses or sheep or curly froth.
Waves that are cold as bare floor, waves that are warm as toast.
There are waves called the Black Sea, the Red Sea, the North Sea,
Waves called the Pacific ocean, the Atlantic ocean, the Antarctic.
If you counted them all, wave upon wave upon wave
would it be a hundred, a thousand, a billion—or more?

Jackie Kay

WINDRUSH CHILD

Behind you
Windrush child
palm trees wave goodbye

above you
Windrush child
seabirds asking why

around you
Windrush child
blue water rolling by

beside you
Windrush child
your Windrush mum and dad

think of storytime yard
and mango mornings

and new beginnings
doors closing and opening

will things turn out right?
At least the ship will arrive
in midsummer light

and you Windrush child
think of Grandmother
telling you don't forget to write

and with one last hug
walk good walk good
and the sea's wheel carries on spinning

and from that place England
you tell her in a letter
of your Windrush adventure

stepping in a big ship
not knowing how long the journey
or that you're stepping into history

bringing your Caribbean eye
to another horizon
Grandmother's words your shining beacon

learning how to fly
the kite of your dreams
in an English sky

Windrush child
walking good walking good
in a mind-opening
meeting of snow and sun

John Agard

MAMA-WATA

Down by the seaside
when the moon is in bloom
sits Mama-Wata
gazing up at the moon

She sits as she combs
her hair like a loom
she sits as she croons
a sweet kind of tune

But don't go near Mama-Wata
when the moon is in bloom
for sure she will take you
down to your doom.

Grace Nichols

MAWU OF THE WATERS

I am Mawu of the Waters.
With mountains as my footstool
    and stars in my curls
I reach down to reap the waters with my fingers
    and look!, I cup lakes in my palms.
    I fling oceans around me like a shawl
        and am transformed
            into a waterfall.
        Springs flow through me
        and spill rivers at my feet
            as fresh streams surge
                to make seas.

Abena P. A. Busia

SHE, ON THE WAY TO MONK'S HILL

She knows everyone on the way to Monk's Hill,
stops to ask for mangoes—they are growing everywhere
it's almost a crime to pay.

At the overflowing bridge, men wash pink-skinned sweet potatoes
while the river steals a few,
she hollers hello and lets them know, tells me, they'll fetch them later.

Stopping for ginnip breeds nostalgia
of her childhood in Guyana—
plantain, sour-sop, breadfruit—
always free, from neighbours,

says her brother doesn't believe in apples;
he's never seen an apple tree, so doesn't trust the juice.
But her nephew, he eats strawberries in
banana cake and doesn't know the difference.

She careens through mud; a carefree cowboy, calling out the sights,
arms wrapped around her waist, I am a jockey without her reigns,
holding on to every word, bracing at every hurdle.

Blessing Musariri

THE SONG OF THE HIGHWAY
(EXTRACT)

I am the Highway,
Long, white, winding Highway,
Binding coast to coast
And people to people,
I am the spine of the earth.

Over the hills I glide
And then, come swooping down
To some deserted spot.
Over river and lake I stride—
Through farm and field, and town,
Through desert sands, white-hot.

I laugh when the brooklets laugh,
And weep with wayside trees
So bent—so broken by the wind.
Sometimes the birds and flowers
Fill my path with song and bloom;
Sometimes a fragrant breeze
Leaves me drenched with faint perfume.

Pauli Murray

THE RUNAWAY KITE

My kite broke loose on a windy day,
And 'way, 'way up in the air it flew;
And though I've sought for it, far and near,
It has never come back from the lofty blue.
Now where does it stay, and what does it see,
And what all day long does it find to do?

I think that it floats on a snowy cloud
Or jauntily rides on a saucy breeze;
And when it gets weary it flutters down
To the shelter of tall and stately trees;
Or the fairies may use it as a sail
For their fairy barks that patrol the seas.

Jessie Fauset

LATCH KEY KID

My mother loved me so.
I know this because
one of my earliest memories was coming home from school
finding a door key wrapped neatly in a paper towel
beneath the grates of the barbeque grill.
When I stuck that key in the lock and turned the knob,
the smell of cabbage, fried chicken, cornbread, and black-eyed peas
would hook my nostrils, lift me off of my feet and set me down gently.

Momma always left a note:
"I hope you had a good day, baby."
and kept the radio on KPRT, the gospel channel.
Shirley Ceasar, The Mighty Clouds of Joy, sometimes The Canton Spirituals
filled the room with soul, salvation
and my mother's grace.
Her care and kindness came carried on chords, and melodies,
telling me that I'm her favorite . . . because I am.

One day I came home,
Momma had prepared a meal, like always
but there was no note.
I remember it was raining and
the day was not so good
I needed that note, I needed my mother

Maybe she had a busy day
Maybe she didn't get everything done
for herself
So I wrote her a note:
"Dinner was good, Momma. I hope YOU had a great day."
I don't know, still, to this day, if she read it

I hope she knows I appreciated her,
Not just the black-eyed peas, cabbage, and cornbread on weekdays,
I appreciated that she cared enough,
with everything else in her great big world,
to think of me.
(Thank you, Momma.)

Derrick Barnes

SHEA BUTTER MANIFESTO

We, the forgotten delta people,
the dry riverbed people,
hair calling always for rain,
skin turned skyward wishing for clouds,
we stand for blood.
We kneel for water.
For oil, we lay down,
fingers spread, as if in this way
we might skate across the yellow clay of it all
like lagoon insects.

So it is written:
heal yourself, baby.
With the tree and the touch, with the turmeric.
In this world, nothing brittle prevails,
so in this world, grease is a compliment,
no, it's a weapon,
no, it's a dream you had, where it was cold
and your mother, seeing the threat of gray at your elbows
and knowing that ash is the language of the dead
knelt, and put her hands on your face like this
and anointed you a protected child, a hot iron in a place of frost.
Recall this, and
fear no thickness.
Be resurrected, glistening in the story of you.
Be shining.

Eve L. Ewing

BUT WHAT CAN YOU TEACH MY DAUGHTER

What do you mean
no no no no
you don't have the right
to know
how often
have we built each other
as shelters
against the cold
and even my daughter knows
what you know
can hurt you
she says her nos
and it hurts
she says
when she talks of liberation
she means freedom
from that pain
she knows
what you know
can hurt
but what you do
not know
can kill.

Audre Lorde

FROM YOUR AUNTIE, TO MY BEST FRIEND'S KID

The very hardest thing to picture
Is your mum when she was small–
Yes, it's harder than a brand new colour,
The very hardest thing of all.

You can't imagine her hating greens,
You swear she is the broccoli queen,
You are sure she never stayed up late
Because she's always in bed by eight.

Surely she never hated maths,
Surely she never hated baths,
No you will not be deceived,
It's the hardest thing to believe.

And surely mum has never been afraid,
She has absolutely always been brave,
She can't ever have been scared of the dark
Or of the bullies in the park–

Yes it's hard to believe that mum was small–
But I was there, I saw it all!

She hated spinach, she hated sprouts,
Before bed she would stomp and shout,

She hated baths and tricky sums
She didn't understand dads and mums,
She was scared of bullies too,
And of the dark, just like you.

Sometimes we forget
That our mums were children too,
And sometimes mums forget
Who they were before they grew.

So here I am, answering your call,
To remind your mum what it was to be small.

Ella McLeod

BREAKFAST TABLE

Mama serves us coffee
at night. Not because

she wants us to stay awake.
Everyone brings a dream

to the breakfast table. Face

your food, you are
still in the room

enough not to lessen
your body. Of course

I am here anytime
to make more for you

and your friends
and the distance

between houses
is love

David Ishaya Osu

. . . I WRITE

Ms. Hudgins told our class to draft a poem,
but I don't know how to begin   because

I want it to be pretty like them thick oak trees
with long branches that stretch far like hugging arms.
And flowers with big blooming buds that
bees and butterflies can't get enough of.
Blue skies, too, that melt into orange and yellow
when the sun goes to off to sleep.

But truth is, I don't know which words to throw out
or which ones to keep . . .

I hope it doesn't have to rhyme with phrases
that bounce off the page like a hip-hop song.
Ones that got me wanting to party all night long.
Like on Tina's birthday when we
danced so hard had us rubbing sore feet.
Shoot, we were too tired to bob our heads to the beat.

Ms. Hudgins, please don't make me compose no haiku,
cause see—
I'm bad at math and
I'll have to use my fingers
to count syllables.

Ms. Hudgins tells me to close my eyes and imagine
all the stuff I love and oh, whoa,
I taste my momma's cornbread and hear my daddy's laugh
I giggle at my brother's jokes and smirk at my sister's sass.

I dream and think, think and dream of
summer rainstorms, banana pudding, roller-skating,
salty popcorn, loud crickets, trees bending in the wind,
leaves dancing across the road, belting songs offkey.
I put my pencil to the page and . . .

Alicia D. Williams

I AM THE CREATIVITY

I am the dance step
of the paintbrush singing
I am the sculpture
of the song
the flame breath
of words
giving new life to paper
yes, I am the creativity
that never dies
I am the creativity
keeping my people
alive

Alexis De Veaux

I Love the Look of Words

Popcorn leaps, popping from the floor
of a hot black skillet
and into my mouth.
Black words leap,
snapping from the white
page. Rushing into my eyes. Sliding
into my brain which gobbles them
the way my tongue and teeth
chomp the buttered popcorn.

When I have stopped reading,
ideas from the words stay stuck
in my mind, like the sweet
smell of butter perfuming my
fingers long after the popcorn
is finished.

I love the book and the look of words
the weight of ideas that popped into my mind
I love the tracks
of new thinking in my mind.

Maya Angelou

THINGS

Went to the corner
Walked in the store
Bought me some candy
Ain't got it no more
Ain't got it no more

Went to the beach
Played on the shore
Built me a sandhouse
Ain't got it no more
Ain't got it no more

Went to the kitchen
Lay down on the floor
Made me a poem
Still got it
Still got it

Eloise Greenfield

TO THE NOTEBOOK KID

yo chocolate milk for breakfast kid.
one leg of your sweatpants rolled up
scrounging at the bottom of your mama's purse
for bus fare and gum
pen broke and you got ink on your thumb kid

what's good, hot on the cement kid
White Castle kid
tongue stained purple
cussin on the court
till your little brother shows up
with half a candy bar kid

got that good B in science kid
you earned it kid
etch your name in a tree
hug your granny on her birthday
think of Alaska when they shootin
curled-up dreams of salmon
safety
tundra
the farthest away place you ever saw in a book
polar bears your new chess partners
pickax in the ice
Northern Lights kid

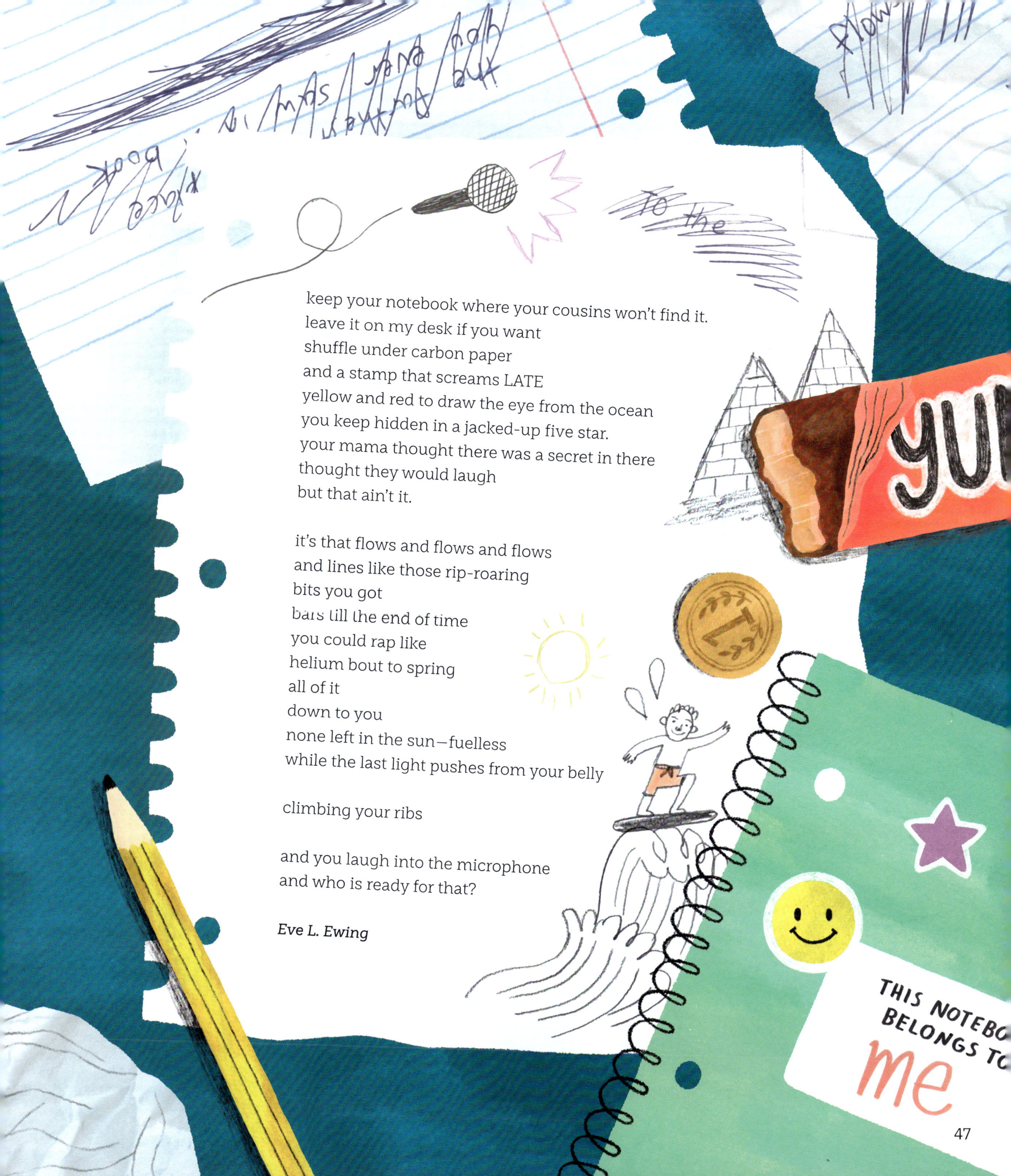

keep your notebook where your cousins won't find it.
leave it on my desk if you want
shuffle under carbon paper
and a stamp that screams LATE
yellow and red to draw the eye from the ocean
you keep hidden in a jacked-up five star.
your mama thought there was a secret in there
thought they would laugh
but that ain't it.

it's that flows and flows and flows
and lines like those rip-roaring
bits you got
bars till the end of time
you could rap like
helium bout to spring
all of it
down to you
none left in the sun—fuelless
while the last light pushes from your belly

climbing your ribs

and you laugh into the microphone
and who is ready for that?

Eve L. Ewing

Delroy
The Skateboard Roller

I dance and dance myself away from here
as a skateboard flyer,
as a boy space-walker,
as a dancer-boy explorer.

In my deep sea gear
I have my deep sea flair.
I do my underwater walk
surrounded by sharks.

And how I spin and wheel round on my top,
how I body-break and body-pop,
people's legs take off on a hop
thinking they can't stop.

And because it's all a body full of joy—
in the boy Delroy
like a man employed—
I am a dancer-boy explorer
a dancer-boy explorer.

James Berry

FOR POETS

Stay beautiful
but don't stay down underground too long
Don't turn into a mole
or a worm
or a root
or a stone

Come on out into the sunlight
Breathe in trees
Knock out mountains
Commune with snakes
& be the very hero of birds

Don't forget to poke your head up
& blink
think
Walk all around
Swim upstream

Don't forget to fly

Al Young

ALLOW ME TO INTRODUCE MYSELF

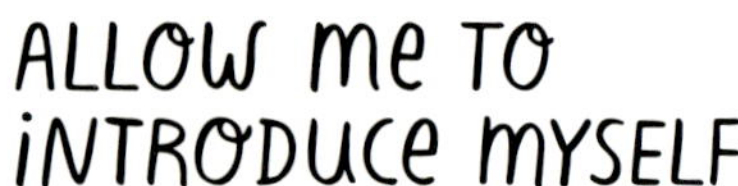

They call me
the show stopper
the dime dropper
the spin-move-to-the-left
reverse jam poppa.
The high flier
on the high wire.
The intense rim-rattlin'
noise
amplifier.

The net-shaker
back board break
creator
of the funk dunk
hip-shaker.
The Man
Sir Slam
The Legend
I be.

That's just
a few of the names
they call me.

Charles R. Smith Jr.

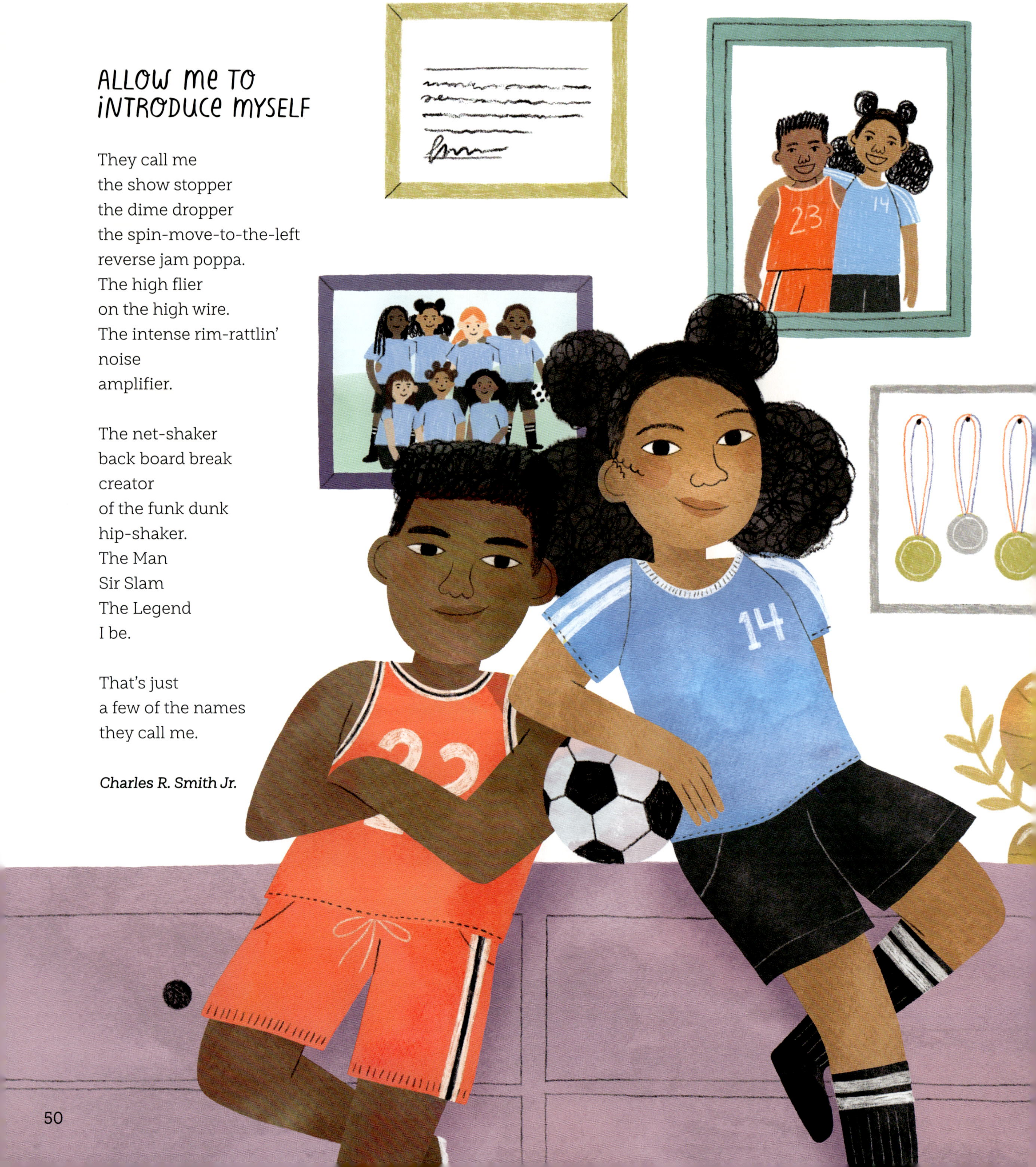

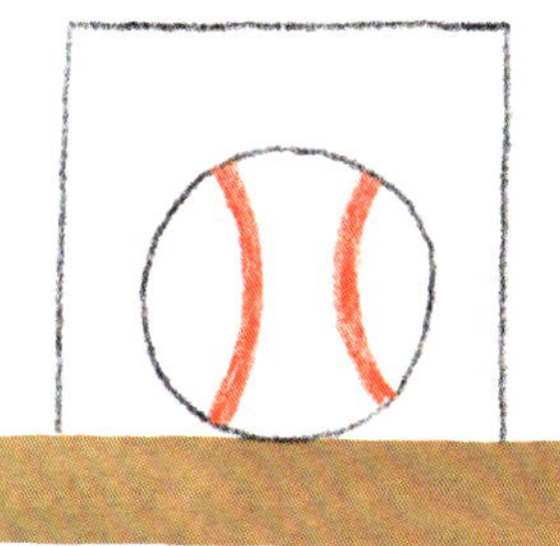

THE EMANCIPATION OF GEORGE-HECTOR (A COLORED TURTLE)

George-Hector
is
spoiled.
formerly he stayed
well up in his
shell . . . but now
he hangs arms and legs
sprawlingly
in a most langorous fashion
head rared back
to
be
admired.

he didn't use to
talk . . .
but
he does now.

Mari Evans

AMERICAN GOTHIC (TO SATCH)

The career of Satchel Paige, the legendary baseball pitcher, extended into five decades.

Sometimes I feel like I will *never* stop
Just go on forever
Till one fine mornin'
I'm gonna reach up and grab me a handfulla stars
Swing out my long lean leg
And whip three hot strikes burnin' down the heavens
And look over at God and say
How about that!

Samuel Allen

SCIENCE...

Science
tells you
Black is the
absence of light
but
your soul
tells you Black
is the light of the
world.

Gordon Nelson

GOOD TROUBLE

Accidental witness,
I watch Black books being
yanked from
school library shelves
like outlaws.
It makes me want to spit.
Instead, I sit
with the anger
until an idea hits me.
Soon as the last bell
puts fire to my feet,
I burn a path
to Mahogany Bookstore,
and flame through the aisles
searching for copies of
New Kid, *The Talk*,
and *Black Boy Joy*.
At checkout, I plunk down
the sneaker money
I've been saving since forever.
Yeah, that means
no new kicks for me
anytime soon.
It's okay, though.
Tomorrow, I'm starting
an after school
banned-book club.
You want to come?

Nikki Grimes

THIS IS NOT A SMALL VOICE

This is not a small voice
you hear   this is a large
voice coming out of these cities.
This is the voice of LaTanya.
Kadesha. Shaniqua. This
is the voice of Antoine.
Darryl. Shaquille.
Running over waters
navigating the hallways
of our schools spilling out
on the corners of our cities and
no epitaphs spill out of their river
mouths.

This is not a small love
you hear   this is a large
love, a passion for kissing learning
on its face.
This is a love that crowns the feet
with hands
that nourishes, conceives, feels the
water sails
mends the children,
folds them inside our history
where they
toast more than the flesh
where they suck the bones of the
alphabet
and spit out closed vowels.
This is a love colored with iron
and lace.
This is a love initialed Black
Genius.

This is not a small voice
you hear.

Sonia Sanchez

SILENT TALKING

I didn't talk much today.
Those who did all the talking kept asking
"are you okay?"
Kept asking "why are you so quiet?"
In my head I answered . . .

There is power in silence.
There is strength in silence.
There is learning in silence.
There is renewal in silence.
There is solitude and safety in silence.

There is hearing in silence.
There is healing in silence.
There is knowing in silence.
There is mystery in silence
    and mysteries are solved in silence.

There is peace in silence.
There is grief in silence.
There is growth in silence.
There is hope in silence.

There are dreams in silence.
There is creativity in silence.
There is music and madness in silence.

There is vision in silence.
There is joy in silence.
There are words and sentences,
    and chapters and books, in silence.

There is insight in silence.
There is passion in silence.
There is fantasy in silence.
There is love in silence.
There are memories in silence.
There is movement and rhythm
    and colour, in silence.

There is breath in silence.
There is life and death in silence.

Sometimes my spirit leads me into silence.
I dare to embrace it.
If you need to question it.
    I will answer.
In silence.

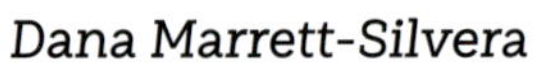
Dana Marrett-Silvera

HAIKU 369

A tall sunflower
And a grinning little boy
With snaggled teeth.

Richard Wright

PHOTOGRAPH

my grandsons
spinning in their joy

universe
keep them turning   turning
black blurs against the window
of the world
for they are beautiful
and there is trouble coming
round and round and round

Lucille Clifton

TOWARD THE SKY

The elm tree boughs grow very high,
And though I stretch up toward the sky,
They're always farther, far, than I,
But yet, as evening shadows fall,
The elm tree boughs that seemed so tall
Lie printed in a pattern, neat,
In gray-blue shadows by my feet.

Effie Lee Newsome

THIRTEEN

You will be four minutes from home
when you are cornered by an officer
who will tell you of a robbery, forty
minutes ago in the area. *You fit*
the description of a man?—You'll laugh.
Thirteen, you'll tell him: you're thirteen.

You'll be patted on the shoulder, then, by another fed
whose face takes you back to Gloucester Primary School,
a Wednesday assembly about being *little stars*.
This same officer had an horizon in the east
of his smile when he told your class that
you were all *supernovas*,
the biggest and brightest stars.

You will show the warmth of your teeth
praying he remembers the heat of your supernova;
he will see you powerless—plump.
You will watch the two men cast lots for your organs.

Don't you remember me? you will ask.
You gave a talk at my primary school.
While fear condenses on your lips,
you will remember that Wednesday, after the assembly,
your teacher speaking more about supernovas:
how they are, in fact, dying stars
on the verge of becoming black holes.

Caleb Femi

A SMALL NEEDFUL FACT

Is that Eric Garner worked
for some time for the Parks and Rec.
Horticultural Department, which means,
perhaps, that with his very large hands,
perhaps, in all likelihood,
he put gently into the earth
some plants which, most likely,
some of them, in all likelihood,
continue to grow, continue
to do what such plants do, like house
and feed small and necessary creatures,
like being pleasant to touch and smell,
like converting sunlight
into food, like making it easier
for us to breathe.

Ross Gay

HAIKU 694

It was so silent
That the silence protested
With one lone bird cry.

Richard Wright

FURY & FAITH
(EXTRACT)

Black lives matter,
No matter what.
Black lives are worth living,
Worth defending,
Worth every struggle.
We owe it to the fallen to fight,
But we owe it to ourselves to never stay kneeling
When the day calls us to stand.

Together, we envision a land that is liberated, not lawless.
We create a future that is free, not flawless.
Again & again, over & over,
We will stride up every mountainside,
Magnanimous & modest.
We will be protected & served
By a force that is honored & honest.
This is more than protest
    It's a promise.

Amanda Gorman

A TRIBUTE

This is for the brothas and sistas
Who ain't here.
To those who have passed on
Their unfinished work to us.

For the stargazers,
The freedom lovers,
The peacemakers,
And my good friend Malcolm,
This one's for you.

This is for the brothas and sistas
Who ain't here.
For the life givers,
For the revolution makers,
The story writers,
And the rhythm shakers,
To you, I say, "Thank you."

This is for the brothas and sistas
Who ain't here.
To you my beloved brothas and sistas
Who have not been given
Your respect due,
Rest in Peace.
Your work shall not be in vain.

Donna F. Thomas

YOU ARE ON YOUR WAY TO GREATNESS

You are on your way to greatness.
Right now, you determine how you will get there,
how you will impact the world.

Right now, you are a star shining beautifully bright.
A descendant from lineages of great people.
People who are strong and bold and brave and resilient.
People who birthed nations,
created civilizations of dreamers,
teachers with hope for a better future.

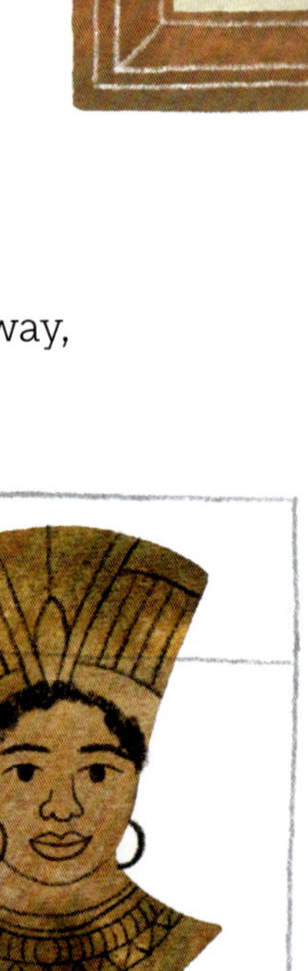

Your ancestors ruled and reigned,
commanded and conquered,
instilled and inspired hope in every cell of humanity.
And one day, you will do the same.

Faith is your vessel, your transportation on a pioneering pathway,
on the *make-a-difference-in-the-world* highway.
Whether there's a stethoscope around your neck,
or a whiteboard at your fingertip,
whether there are briefs to briefly deliver
a summation before the judge and the jury,
or hammer, chisel, and clay before you,
your destiny is greatness.

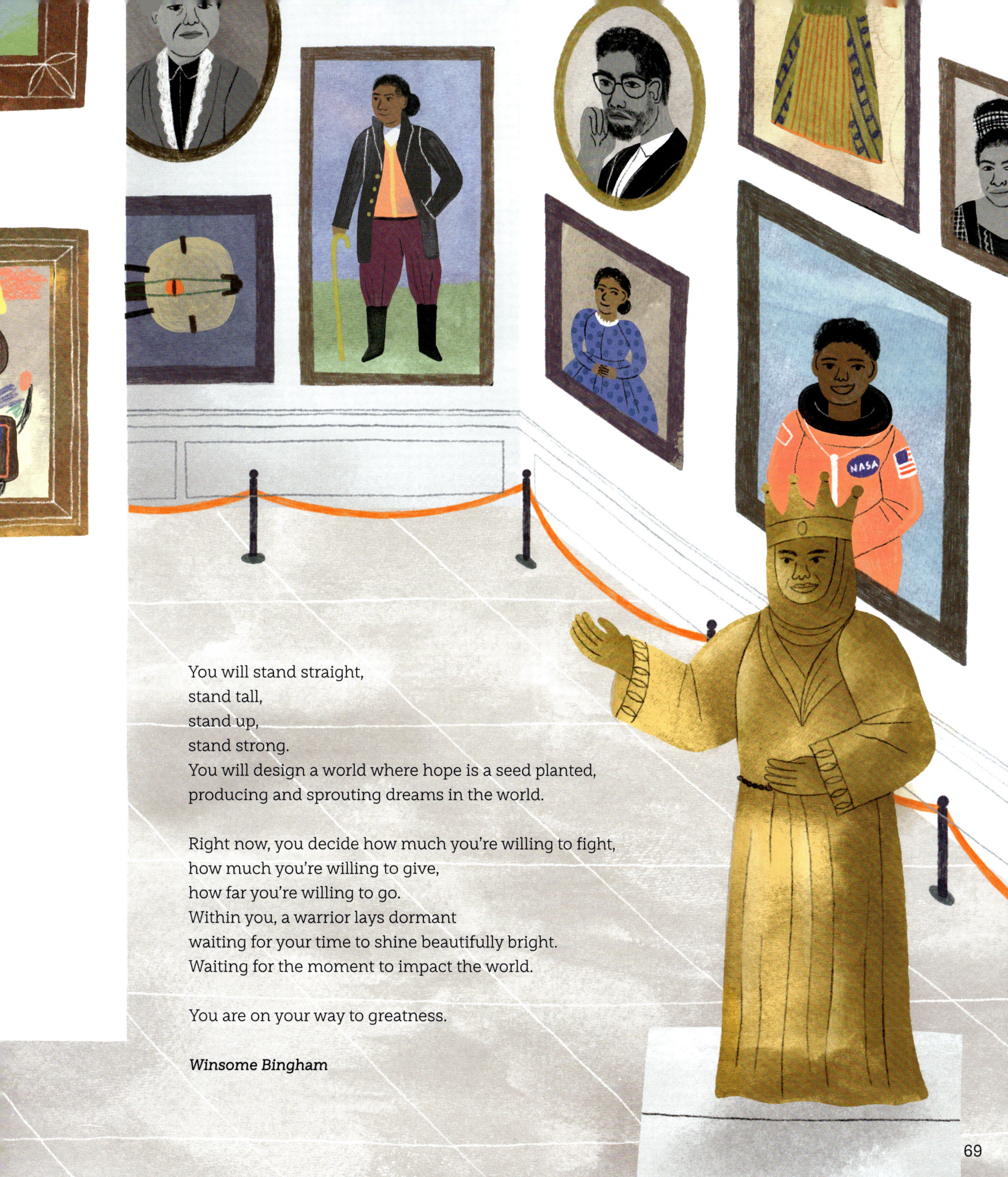

You will stand straight,
stand tall,
stand up,
stand strong.
You will design a world where hope is a seed planted,
producing and sprouting dreams in the world.

Right now, you decide how much you're willing to fight,
how much you're willing to give,
how far you're willing to go.
Within you, a warrior lays dormant
waiting for your time to shine beautifully bright.
Waiting for the moment to impact the world.

You are on your way to greatness.

Winsome Bingham

SAY HOW YOU FEEL

When I'm sad
it feels like the sky is crashing down,
like the oceans are rising
and the ground is swallowing me up.
All is dark and cold.

When I'm nervous
it feels like my heart
is going to lightning-strike out of my chest,
like my skin is raining,
like my belly is a mudslide.

When I'm happy
my cheeks feel like rose buds,
my tummy glows with sunlight,
my shoulders are a forest breeze.

When I'm angry
my body is a rock,
my face is wet clay.
Meteorites inhabit my fists,
my voice is all smoke and fire.

When I'm excited
my toes are ants,
I'm a river bubbling
and an air current of wishes,
my smile could explode the sun.

Joseph Coelho

COMMON THINGS

I love to sit in forests green
'Mid tufts of grass in splendor seen,
And scent the flowers in the air,
And gaze with wond'ring, raptured stare
On common things.

I love to haunt the woodland stream
Where water-lilies paint the scene,
Where meadow-sweet and water-cresses
Add color to the stream's recesses,
Where poppies red, in glory swaying,
Are with the yellow loose-stripes playing;
And then I pause, and think, and ponder,
And soon my heart is filled with wonder
At common things.

I love to hear a passing bird
Trill notes the sweetest ever heard!
I love to hear the night-bird's screeches,
Or watch the squirrel in the beeches;
Each sight, each sound a new joy teaches
In common things.

James Alpheus Butler, Jr.

October
(Extract)

Stay,
you are beginning to glow

I still have
some poems to feed you.

Ijeoma Umebinyuo

I THINK I'LL CALL IT MORNING

I'm gonna take myself a piece of sunshine
and paint it all over my sky.
Be no rain. Be no rain.
I'm gonna take the song from every bird
and make them sing it just for me.
Be no rain.
And I think I'll call it morning from now on.
Why should I survive on sadness,
convince myself I've got to be alone?
Why should I subscribe to this world's madness,
knowing that I've got to live on?
I think I'll call it morning from now on.
I'm gonna take myself a piece of sunshine
and paint it all over my sky.
Be no rain. Be no rain.
I'm gonna take the song from every bird
and make them sing it just for me.
Why should I hang my head?
Why should I let tears fall from my eyes
when I've seen everything that there is to see
and I know that there ain't no sense in crying!
I know that there ain't no sense in crying!
I think I'll call it morning from now on.

Gil Scott-Heron

HAIKU

Let me wear the day
Well so when it reaches you
You will enjoy it.

Sonia Sanchez

MORNING

Day came in
on an old brown bus
with two friends.
She crept down
an empty street
bending over
to sweep the thin dawn away.
With her broom,
she drew red streaks
in the corners
of the dusty sky
and finding a rooster still asleep,
prodded him into song.
A fisherman,
not far from the shore,
lifted his eyes, saw her coming,
and yawned.
The bus rolled by,
and the two friends caught
a glimpse of blue
as day swung around a corner
to where the sea met a road.
The sky blinked,
woke up,
and may have changed its mind,
but day had come.

Dionne Brand

CARNIVAL DAYS
(EXTRACT)

On days like these we dance to us,
With the drum beat of liberation
Under the close cover of European skies,
We dance like true survivors
We dance to the sounds of our dreams.
In the mirror we see
Rainbow people on the beat,
Everyday carnival folk like we.

Adorned in the colours of life
We let it be known that our costumes
Were not made by miracles,
We are the miracles
(And we are still here).
These giants were made by the fingers you see
(Too many to count)
Carried by these feet that dance
In accordance to the rhythms we weave.
On days like these we dance the moon.

Benjamin Zephaniah

WHERE THE RAINBOW ENDS

Where the rainbow ends
There's going to be a place, brother,
Where the world can sing all sorts of songs,
And we're going to sing together, brother,
You and I, though you're white and I'm not.
It's going to be a sad song, brother,
Because we don't know the tune,
And it's a difficult tune to learn.
But we can learn, brother, you and I.
There's no such tune as a black tune.
There's no such tune as a white tune.
There's only music, brother,
And it's music we're going to sing
Where the rainbow ends.

Richard Rive

A RAINY DAY

Outside I hear the dashing rain
Fall full against the window pane.
On such a day, the fire aglow,
An easy chair, a book or so,—
What more would I that fortune bring?
Yet hark! I hear a step—a ring—
And close to heart and hearth I fold
My friend, who guessed my wish untold.
For other joys I do not pray,
Content am I this rainy day.

Lottie Burrell Dixon

THE COTTON CAT

With button eyes and cotton skin
How can a kitten sit and grin?
With skin of striped calico
And only thread between each toe—
I've looked and found out, so I know!

It must feel funny for a cat
To have its tail just painted flat.
But when we're in because of snow
I hold my toy at the window,
And I forget the button eyes
As we both watch the storm and skies.

Effie Lee Newsome

HAIKU 457

A railroad station:
A crowd of summer children
Laughing in the rain.

Richard Wright

WINTER POEM

once a snowflake fell
on my brow and i loved
it so much and i kissed
it and it was happy and called its cousins
and brothers and a web
of snow engulfed me then
i reached to love them all
and i squeezed them and they became
a spring rain and i stood perfectly
still and was a flower

Nikki Giovanni

SNOW PRINTS

Along the paths my overshoes
Make little pits in twos and twos.
But often on that very day
The sunshine melts them all away.

It seems a funny kind of waste,
These footprints getting all erased.
It takes a very icy day
To ever really make them stay.

Effie Lee Newsome

FROM SPACE

Seen from space
our planet is
a blue marble,
tiny and vulnerable,
a child's plaything.

When giants play at marbles
the marbles often crack.
A crack for all the plastic
clogging up the seas.
A crack for all the pollution,
a crack for the felling of trees.
A crack for all the oil
that spills and coats and chokes,
a crack for every politician
who says global warming's a joke.

Seen from space
our planet is
a teary eye,
sad and soft,
begging to be wiped.

When tears are left to pool
sadness drowns us all . . .
A tear for the crops
that can no longer flourish and grow.
A tear for every child
who will never get to grow old.
A tear for every bullet,
every bomb
that should never have been made.
A tear for the next generation
who never asked to play this game.

Given a little space,
could the planet heal?

Space for the fish
to repopulate the seas.
Space for the forests
to once again know trees.
Space for the skies to cry away the smoke.
Space for the next generation
to fix what their forefathers broke.

Joseph Coelho

APOLLO

We pull off
to a road shack
in Massachusetts
to watch men walk

on the moon. We did
the same thing
for three two one
blast off, and now

we watch the same men
bounce in and out
of craters. I want
a Coke and a hamburger.

Because the men
are walking on the moon
which is now irrefutably
not green, not cheese,

not a shiny dime floating
in a cold blue,
the way I'd thought,
the road shack people don't

notice we are a black
family not from there,
the way it mostly goes.
This talking through

static, bounces in space-
boots, tethered
to cords is much
stranger, stranger

even than we are.

Elizabeth Alexander

WHERE'S MY MOON?

Gazing at the sky, all cloud-strewn
A child wonders, *Where's my moon?*

Child cries a river like a monsoon;
Wails and wails, *Where's my moon?*

Tucked in bed, snug as a cocoon,
Child coos gently, *Where's my moon?*

Child wakes at sun up, fresh as June
But worries still, *Where's my moon?*

Child nibbles fruit like a little raccoon;
Frets between bites, *Where's my moon?*

Child even watches a favorite cartoon.
But her mind wanders: *Where's my moon?*

Like a broken record stuck on one tune,
Child keeps asking, *Where's my moon?*

Child makes pretend all afternoon
And quizzes a wizard, *Where's my moon?*

Child swims long and wrinkles like a prune;
Floats the question, *Where's my moon?*

Child's dinosaur twisted from a green balloon
Pop! Gone forever. *Like my moon?*

Child eats ice cream from a silver spoon.
The scoop a reminder: *Where's my moon?*

Child rolls in the tub like a silly loon.
Splashing, asking, *Where's my moon?*

Child sees the sunset from her little room,
and begs once more: *Where's my moon?*

Mama promises, *Soon, dear, soon.*
And sure enough: *There's my moon!*

Carole Boston Weatherford

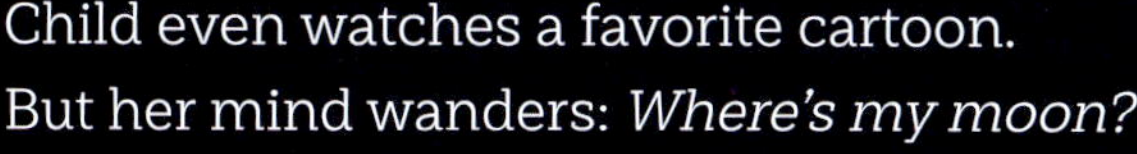

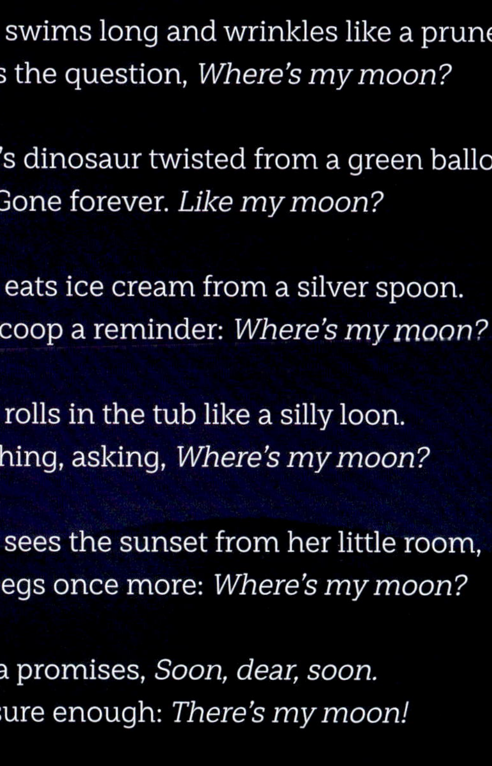

GRANDDADDY

Nobody has a granddaddy
like my granddaddy.
Nobody's granddaddy is named
Douglas Richie Blue.
Nobody's grandfather
has smoked a pipe for fifty years
and always has tobacco to chew.
Nobody else's Big Daddy
can carve whistles out of wood.
Nobody else's grandfather
has feet almost two feet long.
Only my grandpa
can catch fifteen fish in a day.
And he makes up his very own silly songs.

Nobody has a granddaddy
like my granddaddy.
Nobody has a heart
as big as his.

Dinah Johnson

TIMMY AND TAWANDA

It is a marvelous thing and all
When aunts and uncles come to call.
For when our kin arrive (all dressed,
On Sunday, in their Sunday-best)
We two are almost quite forgot!
We two are free to plan and plot.
Free to raid Mom's powder jar;
Free to tackle Dad's cigar
And scatter ashes near and far;
Free to plunder apple juice;
Let our leaping Rover loose.
Lots of lovely things we two
Plot and plan and quickly do
When aunts and uncles come to call,
And rest their wraps in the outer hall.

Gwendolyn Brooks

BEING BLACK IN MY NEIGHBORHOOD

Being Black in my neighborhood
Is a splendid thing
Like bright sunshine
And new clothes in Spring.

We got our own special ways
And our own special days,

Like Sunday morning.
Now that's a time
For colored boys and girls
To put on clothes as they say
And pose and strut,
Boys in their three piece suits,
Clean,
Know what I mean,
And girls so shiny
Hair greased back, with pretty curls
And bows and braids.
Ah, the whole neighborhood
Is laid.
Use to even be hats
And white patent leather pocketbooks
For handkerchiefs only.

Being Black in my neighborhood
Is a splendid thing,
Like singing in the Summer
On the corner
Under the moth encircled
Lamppost.

Oh, what joy it is
On my block
Being Black.

Ja A. Jahannes

SCHOOL
HEY

PLAY SONG

Let's go up to the hillside today
to play, to play
to play.

Up to the hill where the daisies grow
like snow, like snow
like snow.

There we shall make a daisy chain
One tomorrow and tomorrow again
There where the daisies grow like snow
There's where we will go.

Let us go down to the little bay
to play, to play
to play.

Down to the bay where the children swim,
like fish, like fish
like fish.

Down to the bay where the children swim,
Down to the bay where the white yachts skim,
Or up to the hill where the daisies grow,
There's where we will go.

Peter Clarke

SALT! VINEGAR! MUSTARD! PEPPER!

Spring evenings after supper
When we're all dressed up so neat,
We children take our skipping-rope
And play out in the street.
You never heard such noise and mirth,
Or saw such nimble feet.
We jump all sorts of fancy ways,—
"High water, water low",
And some of us jump "Double Dutch",—
We do it fast or slow;
But "Vinegar, mustard, pepper, salt!"
Is the favorite, you know.

Jessie Fauset

IRIS SONG

You go outside and the trees don't know
You're black. The lilacs will chatter and break
Themselves real bloom, real boon,
No matter your gender. You matter.
Who in you is most material, so
You matter. Your afro gone touch the sky.
Come up from the ground looking extra fly,
Come up from the ground looking extra, fly,
I will touch the sky. I—open my mouth,
And my whole life falls out.

Rickey Laurentiis

WHO CAN BE BORN BLACK

Who
can be born black
and not
sing
the wonder of it
the joy
the
challenge

And/to come together
in a coming togetherness
vibrating with the fires of pure knowing
reeling with power
ringing with the sound above sound above sound
to explode/in the majesty of our oneness
our comingtogether
in a comingtogetherness

Who
can bc born
black
and not exult!

Mari Evans

CLIMBING TOGETHER

I'm a long way up and it's almost like the air
pushes back with each step forward I take.
I am hiking up the mountainside.
I have my family in front of me,
and I have my family behind me.
I know that where we're going is worth it—
We are headed to the summit.
On the way up I can see a beetle in the dry dirt
beside my shoes, and white butterflies fluttering
in the purple flowers. A chipmunk moves along
a highway of branches. They move as I move,
with purpose and curiosity. When we reach the top,
I let out a sing-songy exhale and I feel proud.
From here, I can see farther and in some ways, more:
the peaks and slopes of hillsides, a blanket of rockface.
And in other ways I can see less: no beetles,
and no butterflies. Whatever I can see,
my family can also see. And maybe what I'm feeling,
they're feeling too. We take it all in.
And then we head back down.

Rio Cortez

HISTORY LESSON

I am four in this photograph, standing
on a wide strip of Mississippi beach,
my hands on the flowered hips

of a bright bikini. My toes dig in,
curl around wet sand. The sun cuts
the rippling Gulf in flashes with each

tidal rush. Minnows dart at my feet
glinting like switchblades. I am alone
except for my grandmother, other side

of the camera, telling me how to pose.
It is 1970, two years after they opened
the rest of this beach to us,

forty years since the photograph
where she stood on a narrow plot
of sand marked *colored*, smiling,

her hands on the flowered hips
of a cotton meal-sack dress.

Natasha Trethewey

GRITS: 1967

Nana's kitchen
is as old as the Civil Rights Movement,
sometimes she can't remember
which came first,
the grits,
or the riots.

Jasmine Mans

GREENS

Lid's on, steam's risin':
collard greens, Lord, bubblin' JAZZ!
That's appetizin'.

James A. Emanuel

MAMMIE'S COO-COO AND CALLALOO

Every Sunday
Mammie cook coo-coo and callaloo.

Sometimes, there's
peas and rice and salt-beef stew;

I don't know what I would do
without Mammie's coo-coo and callaloo.

Sometimes there's
chicken with pumkin and dasheen too;

I don't know what I would do
without Mammie's coo-coo and callaloo.

Sometimes, there's
pelau, and on the side spicy manicou;

I don't know what I would do
without Mammie's coo-coo and callaloo.

Sometimes there's
poun plantain with curried cascadoo;

I don't know what I would do
without Mammie's coo-coo and callaloo.

Mmmmm, mmmmm I would like some now.
Would you like some too
of Mammie's coo-coo and callaloo?

Yeeeeeeesssssss!!!

I don't know what I would do
without Mammie's coo-coo and callaloo.

John Lyons

JAMAICA MARKET

Honey, pepper, leaf-green limes,
Pagan fruit whose names are rhymes,
Mangoes, breadfruit, ginger-roots,
Granadillas, bamboo-shoots,
Cho-cho, ackees, tangerines,
Lemons, purple Congo-beans,
Sugar, akras, kola-nuts,
Citrons, hairy coconuts,
Fish, tobacco, native hats,
Gold bananas, woven mats,
Plantains, wild-thyme, pallid leeks,
Pigeons with their scarlet beaks,
Oranges and saffron yams,
Baskets, ruby guava jams,
Turtles, goat-skins, cinnamon,
Allspice, conch-shells, golden rum.
Black skins, babel—and the sun
That burns all colours into one.

Agnes Maxwell-Hall

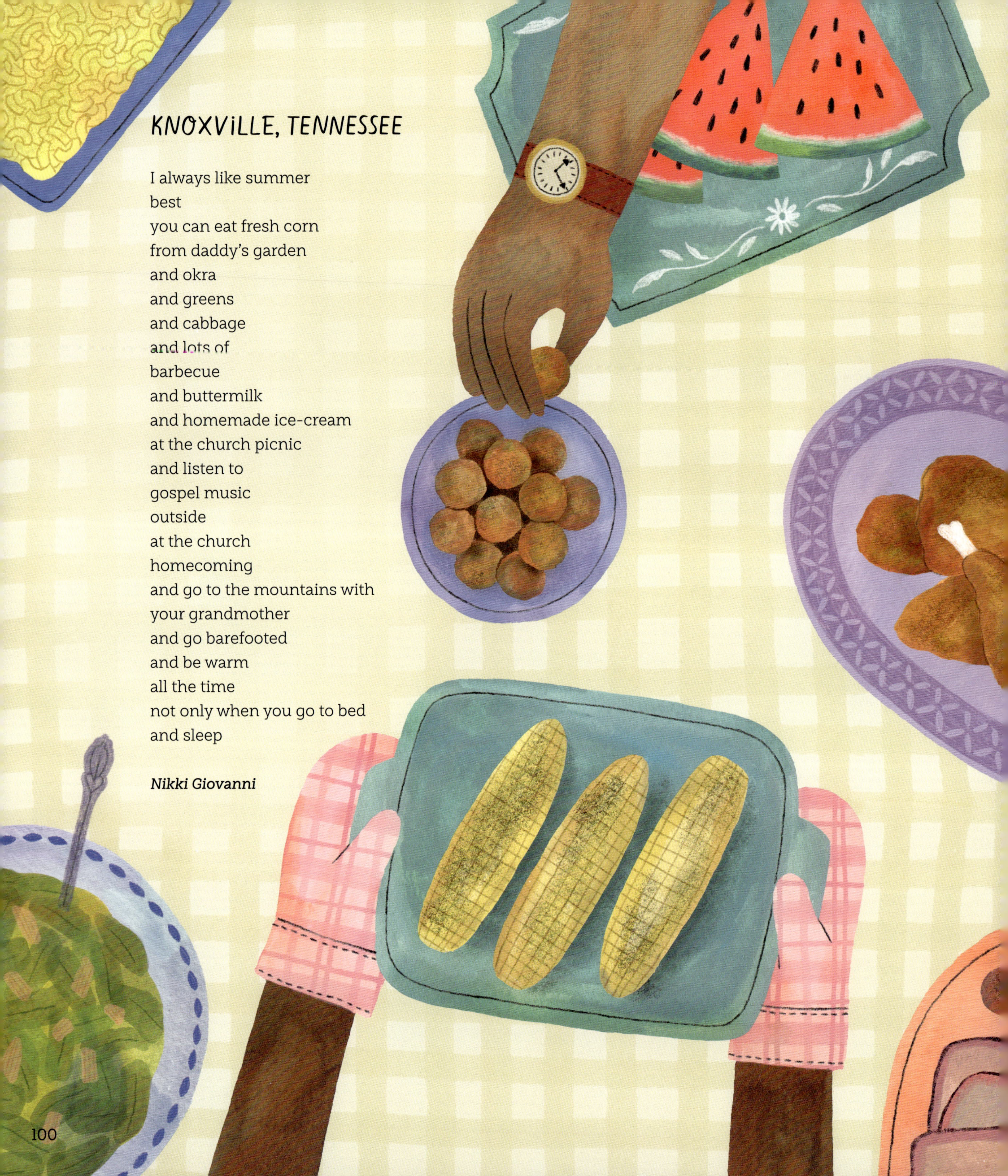

KNOXVILLE, TENNESSEE

I always like summer
best
you can eat fresh corn
from daddy's garden
and okra
and greens
and cabbage
and lots of
barbecue
and buttermilk
and homemade ice-cream
at the church picnic
and listen to
gospel music
outside
at the church
homecoming
and go to the mountains with
your grandmother
and go barefooted
and be warm
all the time
not only when you go to bed
and sleep

Nikki Giovanni

IN PRAISE OF OKRA

No one believes in you
like I do. I sit you down on the table
& they overlook you for
fried chicken & grits,
crab cakes & hush puppies,
black-eyed peas & succotash
& sweet potatoes & watermelon.

Your stringy, slippery texture
reminds them of the creature
from the movie *Aliens*.

But I tell my friends if they don't like you
they are cheating themselves;
you were brought from Africa
as seeds, hidden in the ears and hair
of slaves.

Nothing was wasted in our kitchens.
We took the unused & the throwaways
& made feasts;
we taught our children
how to survive,
adapt.

So I write this poem
in praise of okra
& the cooks who understood
how to make something out of nothing.
Your fibrous skin
melts in my mouth—
green flecks of flavor,
still tough, unbruised,
part of the fabric of earth.
Soul food.

January Gill O'Neil

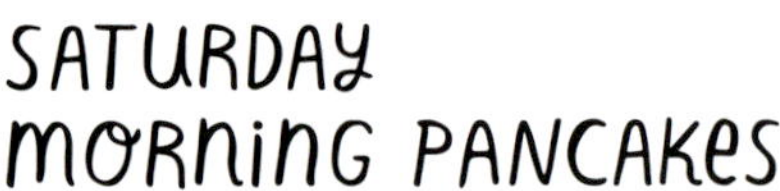

SATURDAY MORNING PANCAKES

In his kitchen
STANDING TALL
flipping pancakes high
in the air
for his captive audience
4 little girls giggling
mesmerized
as Daddy performed
stacking up
golden-brown pride
maple-coated dreams
wishing every day
was Saturday.

Paula White-Jackson

ODE TO A DOMINICAN BREAKFAST

Keep your pancakes, french toast, eggs
benedict, your muffins and scones

Keep your waffles and four types of syrup
the way your eggs scramble but never sizzle

Nothing more scrumptious than mangu con queso frito

The other day I wore a white dress
with a wide skirt and a red sash

I danced merengue barefoot on my stoop. I kissed the
Dominican flag, once for each time I remembered a taino word

yuca, batata, tanama, ocama, yautia, cacique, juracan,
every bite on the plate, every morsel like a bachata tune

This can all be yours, get off the long lines at the brunch spot
forget the grits and cheesy okra. Ring my doorbell

Five ingredients: Olive oil, onions, plantain, white cheese and flour

Yesenia Montilla

ON QUIET FEET

When my dad walks
into a room,
or down
the street,
he inches
up on me
silent
as shadow,
and I don't know
he's there
until I feel
his hug.
Sometimes
when he is
near
I might even
hear
his heart beat—
but never
his quiet
feet.

Nikki Grimes

IN DADDY'S ARMS

in daddy's arms i am tall
& close to the sun & warm
in daddy's arms

in daddy's arms
i can see over the fence out back
i can touch the bottom leaves of the big magnolia tree
in Cousin Sukie's yard
in daddy's arms

in my daddy's arms the moon is close
closer at night time when i can almost touch it
when it grins back at me from the wide twinkling skies

in daddy's arms i am tall
taller than Benny & my friends Ade & George
taller than Uncle Billy
& best of all
i am eye-ball-even-steven with my big brother Jamal

in my daddy's arms
i am strong & dark like him & laughing
happier than the circus clowns
with red painted grins
when daddy spins me round & round
& the whole world is crazy upside down
i am big and strong & proud like him
in daddy's arms
my daddy

Folami Abiade

HAPPY BIRTHDAY MOON

Dad reads aloud. I follow his finger across the page.
Sometimes his finger moves past words, tracing white space.
He makes the Moon say something new every night
to his deaf son who slurs his speech.

Sometimes his finger moves past words, tracing white space.
Tonight he gives the Moon my name, but I can't say it,
his deaf son who slurs his speech.
Dad taps the page, says, *try again*.

Tonight he gives the Moon my name, but I can't say it.
I say *Rain-nan Akabok*. He laughs.
Dad taps the page, says, *try again*,
but I like making him laugh. I say my mistake again.

I say *Rain-nan Akabok*. He laughs,
says, *Raymond you're something else*.
I like making him laugh. I say my mistake again.
Rain-nan Akabok. What else will help us?

He says, *Raymond you're something else*.
I'd like to be the Moon, the bear, even the rain.
Rain-nan Akabok, what else will help us
hear each other, really hear each other?

I'd like to be the Moon, the bear, even the rain.
Dad makes the Moon say something new every night
and we hear each other, really hear each other.
As Dad reads aloud, I follow his finger across the page.

Raymond Antrobus

THE GHOSTS OF WOMEN ONCE GIRLS
(EXTRACT)

somewhere a little girl is reading aloud
in the middle of a dirt road. she smiles
at the sound of her own voice escaping
the spine of a book. she feeds on her hunger
to know herself. she has not yet been taught
to dim, she sits with the stars beneath her feet,
a constellation of things to come.

Aja Monet

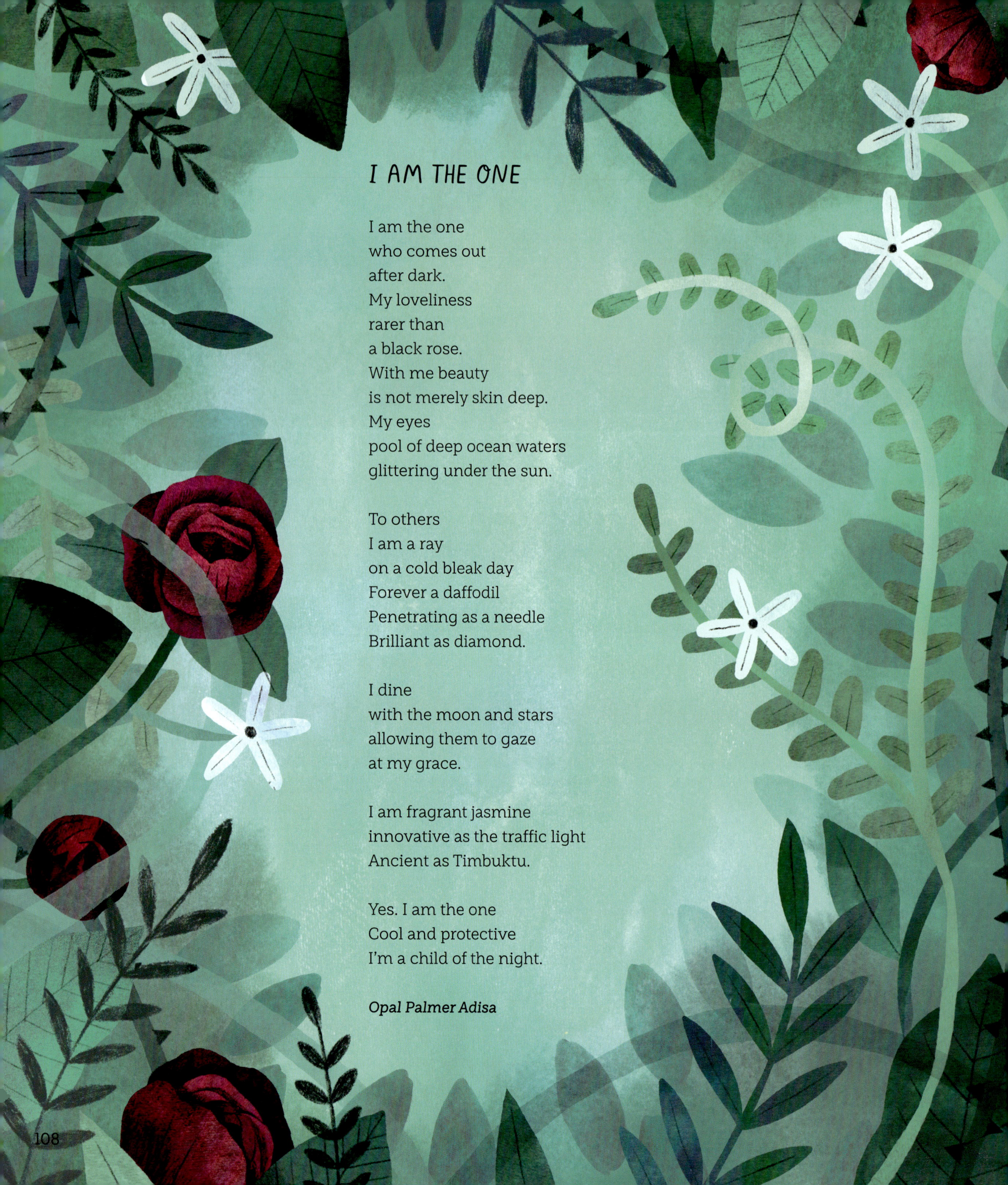

I AM THE ONE

I am the one
who comes out
after dark.
My loveliness
rarer than
a black rose.
With me beauty
is not merely skin deep.
My eyes
pool of deep ocean waters
glittering under the sun.

To others
I am a ray
on a cold bleak day
Forever a daffodil
Penetrating as a needle
Brilliant as diamond.

I dine
with the moon and stars
allowing them to gaze
at my grace.

I am fragrant jasmine
innovative as the traffic light
Ancient as Timbuktu.

Yes. I am the one
Cool and protective
I'm a child of the night.

Opal Palmer Adisa

SPIRIT ENCHANTMENT

Open your ears to spirit sounds
Open your ears to secret words
Open your mind to spirit songs
Open your soul to receive
Spirits of your family
Spirits of your kind
Spirits of yourself
Sounds of the secret places
Songs of the invisible spaces
Come sing the warm songs sung
in the inner self
come sing the warm songs sung
in the inner self
come sing the warm songs sung
in the inner self
Oh . . . help me lawd . . .
sing the warm songs sung
in the inner self
in the inner self
in the inner self
yas . . . indeed . . .

Ed Bullins

FANTASY

I sailed in my dreams to the Land of Night
Where you were the dusk-eyed queen,
And there in the pallor of moon-veiled light
The loveliest things were seen . . .

A slim-necked peacock sauntered there
In a garden of lavender hues,
And you were strange with your purple hair
As you sat in your amethyst chair
With your feet in your hyacinth shoes.

Oh, the moon gave a bluish light
Through the trees in the land of dreams and night.
I stood behind a bush of yellow-green
And whistled a song to the dark-haired queen . . .

Gwendolyn Bennett

NIGHT SONGS

"Pung-la-la," from the frog by my window.
"Shirr-ooo-ooo," from the midnight manicou.
"Ba-lo-ma," from the agouti in the yard.
"Rill-dee-dee," from the mongoose in the tree.
"Gonck-gonck," from the tatou by the pole.
"Urol-el-el," from the matapel.
"Goodnight," I whisper to my moonlight friends
singing their bedtime songs to the sky.

Lynn Joseph

LULLABY

sleep, love, sleep,
just such peace
as you seem
to lie in
there to dream
is my least
gift, love, sleep.

sleep, love, sleep,
while I watch
here close by,
no harm comes,
rest easy,
good dreams catch
you, love, sleep.

sleep, love, sleep,
no thing brings
me greater
comfort than
being here
while your thoughts
sleep, love, sleep.

Quandra Prettyman

THE QUILT

I have the greatest fun at night
When casement windows all are bright.
I play each window is a square
Of some great quilt up in the air,
With bits of light, and dark between,
Wherever only night is seen.

It really makes a mammoth quilt—
With blocks of black and checks of gilt—
That covers up the tired day
In such a cozy kind of way.

Effie Lee Newsome

NIGHT

Night like purple flakes of snow
Falls with ease
Catching on the roofs of houses
In the tops of trees
Down upon the distant grass
And the distant flower
It will drift into this room
In an hour. . . . .

Donald Jeffrey Hayes

POEM

The night is beautiful,
So the faces of my people.
The stars are beautiful,
So the eyes of my people.
Beautiful, also, is the sun.
Beautiful, also, are the souls of my people.

Langston Hughes

AFTERWORD

Many poems in this book refer to important events, places, and people in history. Here are notes on some of the poems that help to explain the stories they tell.

CULTURE & CONNECTION

The story of the African diaspora (the spread of people from their homeland) is a story of the present and the past. It includes those who migrate by choice, and the descendants of those who migrated by force. Enslaved by the British, French, Dutch, and Spanish, they were shipped to Haiti, Cuba, St. Kitts, St. Lucia, Barbados, Jamaica, Antigua, Grenada, Trinidad, Brazil, and the United States. These people were Asante, Ewe, Fante, Akan, Wolof, Fula, Fon, Igbo, Hausa, Bantu, Efik, Yoruba, San, Himba, and Dogon, to name just a few. Each culture has its own languages, its own gods, its own names, its own songs. People belonging to these cultures are still here, in modern-day Senegal, Ghana, Mali, Nigeria, Benin, Angola, Cameroon, and other countries of West and Central Africa, and throughout the world. Some of us still carry the names and customs of our ancestors, and—in the case of okra, yams, peas, and rice—the food. Some of us connect to our past by turning traditional things into something new.

Movement and migration define the Black experience. And when we face injustice in our new homes, our response is revolution, resistance, and rebirth. Revolution like the one led by Toussaint Louverture against the French in Haiti. Resistance, like the way Darcus Howe and Altheia Jones-Lecointe stood up to the British government when they and seven others were arrested for protesting against police violence. Rebirth, like the combination of European music and African rhythms in the US to create jazz.

One of the most powerful ways we resist is through joy. Through celebrations like Carnival and songs and poems like “Lift Every Voice and Sing,” and by honoring our ancestral connections. Here are a few poems that reflect this legacy.

"Carnival Days" **by Benjamin Zephaniah**
Carnival is celebrated in so many different ways in many different places—from Haiti to Brazil. It is a huge, joyful celebration marked by costume, music, and dance, rooted in the traditions of West and Central Africa. The biggest carnival in Europe is Notting Hill Carnival in London, where the poet Benjamin Zephaniah lived.

"Anancy" **by Andrew Salkey**
Stories of the spider god Anancy (who I know as Anansi, and is sometimes called Aunt Nancy) come from the Asante people of West Africa. Anancy's trickster spirit inspired enslaved people to defy their captors by mocking them, running away, and rising up.

"Mama-Wata" **by Grace Nichols**
Mama-Wata is known by many names throughout the African diaspora. She is a water spirit whose West African roots go back thousands of years. Stories about her often merge with European folktales about mermaids.

"Mumble the Magic Words" **by Jabari Asim**
The myth of the flying Africans is referenced in this poem, and perhaps in "Miss Mary Mack Introduces Her Wings." The story has several origins, inspired by Black people escaping American plantations either by running to freedom or taking their own lives. The popular version recorded by writer Virginia Hamilton includes the magic words: *kum kunka yali, kum tambe!*

"She, On the Way to Monk's Hill" **by Blessing Musariri**
Antigua was once the site of more than 150 sugar plantations, worked by thousands of enslaved people. The British forced enslaved people to build forts, including Fort George on Monk's Hill, to protect the wealthy plantation owners. Today the fort is in ruins and in Blessing Musariri's poem, Black people live freely and joyfully in its shadow.

"Ah Was Readin' A Book" **by Valerie Bloom**
Nanny of the Maroons was the leader of a group who escaped enslavement in Jamaica. She guided the Maroons to win a 12-year war against the British.

"Mawu of the Waters" **by Abena Busia**
Mawu is a creator goddess of the Fon and Ewe people in West Africa and in the Vodún religion. Mawu is believed to have created the Earth and all life on it.

"Checking Out Me History" **by John Agard**
John Agard mentions lots of different historical figures. Touissant Louverture was a military leader in the Haitian Revolution (1791-1804), which defeated French colonial rulers and ended slavery on the island. This was the first successful overthrow of a colony by enslaved people in history! Shaka Zulu was a powerful king of the Zulu Kingdom in Southern Africa. "Arawak" and "Carib" are both terms used to describe different cultures of indigenous people from northern South America and the Caribbean, though we now use the word "Kalinago" instead of "Carib." Mary Seacole was a skilled nurse from Jamaica. She served in the Crimean War (1853-1856), bravely nursing British soldiers on the front lines.

POWER & PROTEST

Love is another crucial part of the story of Black people. Love for ourselves and love for each other. Our collective strength moves mountains.

In the US, the work of Black activists led to the end of enslavement in 1865. In the following years, known as Reconstruction, Black Americans had power. They voted for the first time and elected Black leaders. They started businesses and schools. In response, white people in Southern states formed terror groups and passed laws to limit Black freedom, known as Jim Crow laws. Jim Crow laws segregated (separated) Black people from white people. Black schools received less money than white schools. Black people were paid less, forced into undesirable housing, and their right to vote was all but destroyed. Some Black people fled the South to cities like Chicago, New York, and Los Angeles, while others stayed. Everywhere, Black Americans fought back. In the 1950s and 1960s, this fight was known as the Civil Rights Movement. Across the US, people marched and rallied, led by activists such as Martin Luther King, and demanded change.

The 1960s and 1970s in the UK saw the rise of the Black Power Movement. At the time, the term “coloured people” applied to anyone who wasn’t white, including people born in Britain, and immigrants from former and current British colonies in Asia, Africa, and the Caribbean. Housing, jobs, and schools were segregated, and police were often biased and brutal. Black and Asian Britons fought back, letting the UK know they were determined to stay and thrive.

In 2020, after the murders of George Floyd, Breonna Taylor, Tony McDade, and too many others at the hands of police, the US erupted in protest. People all over the world joined in. This global uprising is often called the Black Lives Matter Movement. In response, many organizations in the US and the UK made efforts to welcome and support people from Black, LGBTQ+, disabled, and other underrepresented communities. In 2025, in the face of a largely white, straight, non-disabled backlash, many of these efforts were discontinued in the US. We fight on.

These poems acknowledge our struggle and celebrate love.

"Lift Every Voice and Sing" by James Weldon Johnson
In 1900, James Weldon Johnson was the principal of a school for Black children in Jacksonville, Florida. The children learned this poem with their families, and sang it at a school assembly. When a fire broke out in Jacksonville, firefighters protected only the white homes. Black families fled to other cities, and carried "Lift Every Voice and Sing" with them. In 1919, it was declared the Black National Anthem of the United States.

"A Tribute" by Donna F. Thomas
This poem remembers all those who fought for freedom, unnamed and named, like the activist Malcolm X.

"Thirteen" by Caleb Femi
Caleb Femi explores police bias and the adultification of Black children. This is when Black children are seen as less innocent and more grown up than white children. In the UK, Black people are stopped by police far more often than any other group.

"Good Trouble" by Nikki Grimes
School libraries in the US face book bans, where certain books are removed from the shelves or the curriculum because they touch on topics that make some adults uncomfortable. The banned books are often by Black authors, authors of color, and LGBTQ+ authors.

"Fury & Faith" by Amanda Gorman
The Black Lives Matter (BLM) movement began in 2013. It is an anti-racist movement fighting for Black people's right to safe, joyful lives without discrimination.

"History Lessons" by Natasha Trethewey
This poem describes a beach that was once segregated and how it has changed over time.

"Grits: 1967" by Jasmine Mans
Jasmine Mans references civil rights protests in 1967 in American cities such as Detroit and Newark.

"A Small Needful Fact" by Ross Gay
Eric Garner lost his life in police custody on July 17, 2014. As officers choked him, he repeatedly said, "I can't breathe." What Ross Gay wants you to know in "A Small Needful Fact" is that Eric Garner was a human being whose life mattered.

"Windrush Child" by John Agard
After World War II, there weren't enough workers to rebuild Great Britain. So the UK government invited people in British Caribbean colonies to move to the UK and help. In 1948, hundreds of Afro-Caribbean people arrived on a ship called HMT *Empire Windrush*. Over the next thirty years, thousands more would follow. The new arrivals were not always welcomed. White folks shut them out of jobs they had been promised, and many descendants of the Windrush generation are still fighting for full British citizenship. But because of this migration, there is a vibrant Afro-Caribbean community in the UK. Windrush Day is celebrated every June 22, as an acknowledgment of the amazing achievements and difficult sacrifices of this community.

INDEX OF POETS

INDEX OF POEMS

INDEX OF FIRST LINES

CREDITS

The publisher would like to thank the copyright holders for granting permission to use the following copyright material:

Amanda Gorman. Used by permission of the author. **Eloise Greenfield**: "Things" from *Honey I Love and Other Love Poems*. Copyright © 1978 by Eloise Greenfield. Used by permission of HarperCollins Publishers. **Nikki Grimes**: "Good Trouble" © Nikki Grimes, 2025. "On Quiet Feet" copyright © 1998 by Nikki Grimes. Originally published by Dial Press. Currently published in *Dime a Dozen*. Reprinted by permission of Curtis Brown, Ltd. **Ellen Hagan and Renée Watson**: "This Body II" excerpted from *Watch Us Rise* by Renée Watson and Ellen Hagan. Text Copyright © Renée Watson and Ellen Hagan, 2019, Bloomsbury Publishing, Inc. **Langston Hughes**: "Poem" and "The Dream Keeper" by Langston Hughes, from *The Collected Poems of Langston Hughes* (Alfred A Knopf/Vintage), reproduced by permission of David Higham Associates. **Dinah Johnson**: "Granddaddy" from *In Daddy's Arms I Am Tall: African Americans Celebrating Fathers*, Lee & Low Books 1997, reprinted by permission of the author. **Jackie Kay**: "Waves" by Jackie Kay. Copyright © Jackie Kay, 1992, used by permission of The Wylie Agency (UK) Limited. **Rickey Laurentiis**: "Iris Song" copyright © 2020 by Rickey Laurentiis, reprinted by permission of the author. **Audre Lorde**: "But What Can You Teach My Daughter" from *The Black Unicorn*, Norton 1978, reprinted by permission of Abner Stein Ltd. **John Lyons**: "Mammie's Coo-Coo and Callaloo" from *A Caribbean Dozen: Poems from Caribbean Poets*, Walker Books 1994 © John C. M. Lyons. All rights reserved. **Jasmine Mans**: "Grits: 1967" from *Black Girl, Call Home* by Jasmine Mans, copyright © 2021 by Jasmine Mans. Used by permission of Berkley, an imprint of Penguin Publishing Group, a division of Penguin Random House LLC. All rights reserved. **Ella McLeod**: "From Your Auntie, To My Best Friend's Kid" © Ella McLeod, 2025. **Aja Monet**: "the ghosts of women once girls" from *My Mother Was a Freedom Fighter*. Copyright © 2017 by Aja Monet. Reprinted by permission of Haymarket Books. **Yesenia Montilla**: "Ode to a Dominican Breakfast" by Yesenia Montilla. From *The Pink Box* (2015), Willow Books, reprinted by permission of Aquarius Press. **Pauli Murray**: "Dark Testament" and "The Song of the Highway" copyright © 1970 by the Pauli Murray Foundation, from *Dark Testament and Other Poems* by Pauli Murray. Used by permission of Liveright Publishing Corporation. **Blessing Musariri**: "She, On the Way to Monk's Hill" © Blessing Musariri, reprinted by permission of Accord Literary. **Grace Nichols**: "Don't Cry Caterpillar" from *No Hickory No Dickory No Dock*. Copyright © Grace Nichols 1991. "Granny Granny Please Comb My Hair" from *Come on Into My Tropical Garden*. Copyright © Grace Nichols 1988. "I Like to Stay Up" from *Under the Moon and Over the Sea*. Copyright © Grace Nichols 2002. "Mama-Wata" from *I Have Crossed An Ocean*. Copyright © Grace Nichols 2010. All reproduced with permissions from Curtis Brown Group Ltd on behalf of Grace Nichols. **January Gill O'Neil**: "In Praise of Okra" from *Underlife*. Copyright © 2009 by January Gill O'Neil. Reprinted with the permission of The Permissions Company, LLC on behalf of CavanKerry Press, Ltd. **David Ishaya Osu:** "Breakfast Table" from *When I'm Eighteen*, 2020, reprinted by permission of the author. **Gabriel Ramirez**: "Before Going to the Barbershop" © Gabriel Ramirez 2019, reprinted by permission of the author. **Andrew Salkey**: "Anancy" from *Time for Poetry*, 1988, reprinted by permission of Jason Salkey on behalf of the Andrew Salkey estate. **Sonia Sanchez**: "This Is Not a Small Voice". From *Wounded in the House of a Friend* by Sonia Sanchez. Copyright © 1995 by Sonia Sanchez. "Haiku". From *Morning Haiku* by Sonia Sanchez. Copyright © 2010 by Sonia Sanchez. Reprinted with permission from Beacon Press, Boston. **Charles R. Smith Jr.**: "Allow Me to Introduce Myself". Copyright © Charles R. Smith Jr., reprinted by permission of the author. **Natasha Trethewey**: "History Lesson" from *Domestic Work*. Copyright © 1998, 2000 by Natasha Trethewey. Reprinted with the permission of The Permissions Company, LLC on behalf of Graywolf Press. **Ijeoma Umebinyuo**: Extract from "Morning Liturgy" and extract from "October" from *Questions for Ada*, © Ijeoma Umebinyuo 2015, reprinted by permission of the author. **Alexis De Veaux**: "I am the creativity" copyright © 1993 by Alexis De Veaux; from *Soul Looks Back in Wonder* by Tom Feelings. Used by permission of Dial Books for Young Readers, an imprint of Penguin Young Readers Group, a division of Penguin Random House LLC. All rights reserved. **Alicia D. Williams**: ". . . I Write" © Alicia D. Williams, 2025. **Jamila Woods**: "Bird's Nest" from *Winter Tangerine Review: Hands Up Don't Shoot* © Jamila Woods 2015, reprinted by permission of the author. **Richard Wright**: "Haiku 369", "Haiku 457" and "Haiku 694" from *Haiku: This Other World*, Arcade Publishing 1998. Used with permission of Skyhorse Publishing, Inc. **Benjamin Zephaniah**: "Carnival Days" from *Too Black, Too Strong* (Bloodaxe Books, 2001). Reproduced with permission of Bloodaxe Books.

Every effort has been made to obtain permission to reproduce copyright material, but there may have been cases where we have been unable to trace a copyright holder. The publisher would be happy to correct any omissions in future printings.

TRACI N. TODD

Traci N. Todd is the award-winning author of *Nina: A Story of Nina Simone*, *Holding Her Own: The Exceptional Life of Jackie Ormes*, and *Make a Pretty Sound: A Story of Ella Jenkins—First Lady of Children's Music*. Traci has also been a children's book editor for over 20 years, and is responsible for many successful titles, including the *New York Times*-bestselling *The ABCs of Black History*. Traci writes and edits in Queens, New York, and when she isn't working, she likes to watch scary movies in the dark.

JADE ORLANDO

Jade Orlando is an award-winning illustrator working in Atlanta, Georgia. Her vibrant illustrations are featured in books, apparel, advertising, and licensing, with clients including Hallmark, Simon & Schuster, and the ACLU. Jade lives with her husband, cats, and a greyhound named Petra. When she's not illustrating, you can usually find her curled up with her pets and a really good book.

1ST